Diggin' for Intimacy:

Sex, Sensuality, and Loving God

June 2022

Arlecia Simmons

Diggin' for Intimacy

Copyright © 2021 by Arlecia Simmons

Cover Illustration: Nastasia Reid

Ordering Information:

Quantity sales. Special discounts are available on quantity purchases by corporations, associations, and others. For details, contact the publisher, admin@drlecia.com. Orders by U.S. trade bookstores and wholesalers. Please visit https://drlecia.com/

Printed in the United States of America

Table of Contents

Preface

Acknowledgments

Dedication

1. Uncrowning Daddy's Little Princess

2. Jesus Is My Boo, Or Maybe Not

3. Lessons from The Lion's Den

4. Sorry, J. Lo, My Love Does Cost A Thing

5. The Secrets of the Sheets

6. What Had Happened Was

7. Don't Scroll to Your Death

8. The Soundtrack of Heartbreak

9. Reclaiming My Time

10. Resting My Field: Putting a Pause on Dating to Restore the Nutrients of Your Soul

Epilogue

Diggin' for Intimacy Playlist

Resources

About the Author

Contact the Author

Dedication

For church girls, daddyless daughters, and sisters who have looked for love in all the wrong places.

Acknowledgments

If God sent physical text messages, I'm sure our conversation thread would be filled with, "SMH" responses.

"Why the confused emoji, God?" I would reply.

Nothing in these pages shocked or surprised God, although most of the accounts will shock or surprise readers.

I'm grateful for the support of my family, village of friends, sorors, colleagues, students, and my social media connections who affirm daily that what I have to offer the world is valuable.

I offer forgiveness and thanks to every man who came into my life to teach me a lesson, whether it felt like a blessing or a curse.

I am grateful for every woman who will pick up this book and journey with me on the path to healing and restoration. I honor the girl in every woman who wasn't protected or loved properly. May you feel like you're not alone as you dig for the treasure within your journey.

Preface

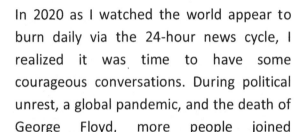

In 2020 as I watched the world appear to burn daily via the 24-hour news cycle, I realized it was time to have some courageous conversations. During political unrest, a global pandemic, and the death of George Floyd, more people joined discussions on social inequities and police brutality. Some conversations were taking place in public that many had shied away from unless behind closed doors.

As we continued to wash our hands, wear masks, and maintain social distance, some public personalities had us talking about romantic "entanglements." Short of calling a relationship a marital affair, one public personality's family saga provided a distraction from the news.

As the global pandemic raged on and I lived in isolation, I began considering my relationship shenanigans that thankfully hadn't played out in the public sphere. But what if they did? What if I talked about those experiences to ignite conversations to be had by individuals during quiet moments of reflection, in sister circles, during church women's conferences, or between lovers who are trying to learn more about their partner's past?

Women often surrender so much emotionally, financially, physically, and sexually in our dating relationships, yet we rarely assess the losses or costs versus the benefits. Books written for and by Christian women often dance around the topic of sensuality and sex, unless it's to advocate for a woman to not engage in intimate exchanges. Purity ceremonies for adult women are still prominent and are now streamed live on platforms like YouTube. But what do you do when you've already done all of what the writers have said *not* to do? How do we process romantic relationships in the community?

What if "church girls" who never lived up to having "no more sheets," finally embraced their sexuality, which led to making healthier decisions regarding love and intimacy?

What if the lessons I've learned from being "tangled up," a time or two, led to someone being delivered from guilt, shame, or possibly self-abuse? Many numb the pain of these experiences with food, shopping, or some form of excess that leaves them feeling broken. But what if digging deeper into past experiences led to recovery, restoration, or even contacting a therapist for more intensive treatment?

For some, this book will begin to transform the way you may see your body, experiences, and your sensuality. For others, it may just inform you to better understand friends, relatives, congregants, or people who complain about their relationship problems. Through my story, you may be able to understand the emotions and exploits they are too embarrassed to share.

This book is for those who never had the space to talk honestly about why they have had sex outside of marriage. However, they embraced religious teachings that left them feeling guilty about the pleasure experienced. The physical pleasure was met by the thought that God was displeased because you had not "kept yourself." It's not the tale of a 45-year-old virgin or the celebration of 20 years of celibacy. This book is for you if you've experienced sexual intimacy but were left wondering if true love would find you.

This book isn't for those who have gotten A's on their relationship report cards. This book was written by someone who has been in remedial courses when it comes to love and relationships. You, the one who said you had cried your last tear only to find yourself ordering a case of tissue online. You, the one who has left things unsaid or said *wayyy* too much. This book is for anyone who believes that God will one day bless you with a mate. No, not a "situationship," or one of the other colloquial words we use to describe our unions. But you are seeking a committed, honest, and God-centered relationship with another human who is not currently committed by marriage or mortgage. Even if you haven't used all of the churchy jargon to describe what you desire and some ratchetness is still your portion, then this book is for you.

This book is for women who are reconciling Paul's admonishment that it is better to marry than burn (1 Corinthians, 7:9) "But where is he, Paul? I'm not trying to burn, but this 'betrothal' you are suggesting isn't happening while something is burning in this body." What happens when marriage doesn't come at 29, 39, 49, or beyond? What happens when you go from hoping, wishing, and praying for your Boaz to only be left disappointed as you find yourself in one broken relationship after another?

If you have been married for most of your adult life and can't understand why some of the younger women around you aren't "trusting God" for their "Boaz," then this book is for you, too. I can't say you will read it and become less judgmental, but you may get a better grasp of what's happening in these Plenty of Fish and eHarmony streets.

For many, this book will be too honest, raw, and transparent because the content does not contain the sanitized testimonies we often share at church during women's conferences or on Saturday at the missionary meeting.

You will listen in on conversations characters like Celie from *The Color Purple* only felt comfortable having with God. I share with you these courageous conversations I've had with God in hopes that you will dig for the treasure of your own past experiences.

Intimacy characterizes close, familiar, and usually affectionate or loving personal relationships and requires the parties to have a detailed knowledge or deep understanding of each other.
—American Psychological Association Dictionary of Psychology

Introduction

*A*fter a prayerful review of a collection of journal entries and stream of consciousness writings, this book was conceived. In these writings, I compiled how I've been able to navigate relationships and sex as a contemporary Christian woman. As a native Gullah Geechee speaker there may be times when my vernacular may change during the narration.

As a heterosexual and cisgender black woman, I share my experiences as a woman who made the decision to engage in sexual relations with men. So, I honestly can't speak for other unions, although the emotional adventure of dating isn't only experienced between men and women.

One of the areas of healing that churches have overlooked is the need to address the issue of sexual assault. While a traumatic encounter may have been some reader's first sexual encounter, such acts of violence are not going to be fully addressed in this book. Because I stumbled into my initial sexual encounters willingly, I grieve for the girls and women who will read this book and may not be able to say the same.

This isn't a discussion in isolation, as many who will pick up this book have already read the book and watched Prophetess Juanita Bynum's *No More Sheets* sermon video from the Woman, Thou Art Loosed conference (circa 1997). After attending that conference or watching the sermon video, women gathered for sheet burning parties, rolled on the floor at smaller conferences, swore off sex, fasted, prayed, and some still left with, "What had happened was..." stories. Fill in the blank. Whether it happened at your house, his house, the hotel, motel, or the car, it's time to begin an honest conversation about sex and sexuality. I know, I know, what's done in the dark needs to stay in the dark. But I believe that what has been done in the dark has impacted our light as we live a life bound in regrets, shame, and framed by rejection. And because we are bound, the generation behind us will make the same mistakes when it comes to dating and sex.

While this book is written from an unmarried woman's experience, I'm sure that others may find some revelation, inspiration, humor, or even some things to add to your prayer list. Prepare to clutch your pearls as we journey together on this talk church girls were often prohibited from having.

What if, instead of making sure I knew *Robert's Rules of Order* or how to line a hymn, discussions were spent helping me and other teenagers understand and explore what our bodies were growing into.

If these conversations weren't happening in the home, then why couldn't the church, the place where I spent the most time in other than school, serve as a space for discussions that could truly set captives free. "Just don't do it," that's the phrase many teen girls of my generation heard without fully knowing exactly what not to do. There were few discussions about our developing bodies, and although those conversations were not had in the home, that may have not stopped those more mature from admiring what was in process.

For those who experienced sexual violence before puberty, how do you undo what was involuntary done to you?

"Doing the do," was something I kind of learned about. I don't recall my own teen mom sitting down and having an in-depth discussion about sex. However, even when we hadn't discussed it with our parents or had a class in school, sex and sexuality are things we rarely get all the information about before voluntarily engaging in a sexual encounter. As soon as we experienced the first signs of something tingling in places we've never experienced before, we were ready to experience what was next.

In some cases, we probably spent more time learning how to get a driver's permit than we did learning how to understand our bodies and what happens during sexual intercourse. And if you were growing up in a Christian home and are an active member of the youth department or the young people's division of your denomination, forget about sex. The expectation is you'll get married and figure it out. Not only will you get married, but whatever goes down on the honeymoon will be a mystery.

For some, the next stop was losing our virginity to the teen boy or grown man who proclaimed his love. For decades, I, like many women, were confused about what was at stake. While pregnancy and sexually transmitted infections (STIs) were the only repercussions loudly noted, the complexity of the emotional toll was never addressed until much later when I concluded:

I don't want lust, I want love.

I don't want a situationship.

I don't want an entanglement.

I want to know the love that comes through effective communication, fellowship, emotional intimacy, and trust. But apparently, I didn't get the syllabus, training manual, or lectures to obtain the love I desired without exchanging physical intimacy. What I did get was practicum hours in heartbreak, frustration, calls from other women, and the shame of never being chosen.

As I learned at an early age, *"He who finds a wife finds a good thing."* (Proverbs 18:22 NKJV). Apparently, I am not a good thing since I haven't been found. Although an uncomfortable truth, it's a reality for so many women whose understanding, relationships, and sexuality have been framed through the lens of a narrow and often unexplained theology that didn't make room for my entire being.

These days with additional lived experiences and theological training, I continue to wrestle with my understanding of sex and dating as a Christian woman. I wish I could say I always got it "right."

April 7, 2015 (Age 41) -
From Arlecia's Journal

Some days, I feel like a complete loser because I do not have a relationship. Most days, I'm perfectly fine, but on the days when I feel like a loser, I recount the conversations that others have had with me. The questions posed, asking about my sexuality, and questions alluding to the fact that maybe there is some defect because no one loves me.

One of the most painful conversations I've ever had about this, was a conversation I had with my father. One day, I would pose the question "Daddy have you been praying for my husband?"

His response: I didn't know you wanted a husband. But daddy, did you not ever listen to my concerns and complaints? "All you ever said was you had friends. One time I posed the question and you got upset, so I assumed you didn't want a man."

Questions, concerns, and comments such as that have led me to think I'm defective. That there is something wrong or missing with my life, with my makeup, with my personality, that no one could ever possibly love me or desire to be in a relationship with me. Questions that sound like "What's wrong with you?"

Why aren't you married?
Well, I can't understand why women like yourself aren't married?
Why don't you have children? Questions that question my humanity, my sexuality, my vulnerability, questions that force me to think that I am not worthy or good enough for love.

Chapter One

Uncrowning Daddy's Little Princess

―――――――――〜―――――――――

Who taught you about love? When was the word "lust" introduced into your vocabulary?

Who helped to socially construct what love and relationships looked like before your young eyes? Who were the actors, the antagonists, the victims, and the victors in your love narrative? Who helped to shape both your sensuality and your sexuality?

I pose these questions because many of us didn't end up in broken or fractured relationships by ourselves. Instead, we arrived with moving trucks filled with attitudes and behaviors learned along the way. Even if we had the healthiest of childhoods, not all of the ways the adults in our lives expressed love, were the healthiest displays. Whether you saw your parents display affection, caught them in the act of sex, or thought all of your mother's "friends" were "uncles" because she never wanted to let you know she had a companion, we have learned how to express love from the people who first loved us.

Some of us also learned certain aspects of love from music and television shows. One of the funniest, yet shameful memories of my childhood is participating in a community talent show at age eight or nine and singing Marvin Gaye's hit, "Sexual Healing." I didn't just sing, but I moved my young body better than Beyoncé ever could. I blame my young adult aunt for being the creative director on that project. While the crowd actively cheered me on, did anyone think, "A child shouldn't be singing that song?" Thankfully, I had not yet experienced "sexual healing" nor sexual pain or trauma.

Then there were the times I had to make sense of the duties of Betty Wright's, "Clean Up Woman," and my young mind had to decipher why Shirley and Barbara were going back and forth over a man. In 1973, when I was conceived by my teenage parents, Marvin Gaye's, "Let's Get It On," was on the airways and may have activated that 14-and 17-year-old imagination. I was born the following year.

My father married another woman when I was a toddler, so I don't have any memories of public intimacy shared between my parents. They are friends who respect one another in thoughts, words, and deeds; however, they were not my model for love. While their teenage love story wasn't a "smash and go" situation, I never witnessed them in a relationship beyond co-parenthood.

I grew up in the house with my maternal grandparents; and while they displayed affection and love toward one another, their love languages didn't consist of physical touch. Acts of Service and Gifts are the two languages I saw displayed often. People in their generation - born in the 20's -didn't exhibit PDA the way younger lovers do. It was assumed they loved one another because they co-existed without violence and there was always food, utilities, and even annual travel. By the time I came around, they were in their late forties and early fifties and the house was crowded. They loved one another, but that love was shown in how they cared for one another.

When it came to an image of physical displays of affection, it wasn't until my pre-teen years when a couple from church became my visual relationship goals. Church folks gossiped when the man would rest his hands on his beloved's hips in the pews or at the altar during prayer. Although I was a teenager when they married, I often sensed there was something wrong with the *hateration* of the adults. "Aren't men supposed to hold their wives lovingly and tightly?" I mean, wouldn't it make more sense to witness the expression of love in the pews than seek out the images embedded on BET's *Video Soul* with Donnie Simpson, a popular show in the late 80s.

While many of the other couples around me seemed to operate in two separate universes, this couple represented the Black love now captured in documentaries and promoted on graphic tees. Like most of the teens around me, I had to figure out what love and relationships were all about on my own as I watched family members, their friends, female neighbors, and the older girls at church who I spent countless hours with at choir practice.

"So, what is this love thing all about?"

I knew I didn't want to be the woman whose love could only come and see her late at night, on weekends, or when his wife was out of town. Oh, and I didn't want to be the woman who would call my childhood home asking if anyone had seen her married lover's car. It was a whole mess.

I didn't want to be one of many women a man could swap out like shoes. I didn't want to be the baby mama who had to fuss and fight with other baby mamas or with the baby daddy who didn't come when he promised. I didn't want to be the woman who returned to her hometown annually and spent a few hours with her childhood love or old boyfriend. And while I liked the beat of Gwen Guthrie's, "Ain't Nothing Going on But The Rent," I sensed a purely transactional love would be unfulfilling.

I didn't want the majority of what I had seen, but I wasn't quite sure what relationship I would enter into, since most of what I had witnessed from the unmarried women on the surface appeared exciting but didn't yield the fruit of marriage or public relationships. After growing up and becoming one of many and the woman whose lover only came late in the midnight hour, I realized that maybe instead of watching, I needed to be listening. But who was there to talk directly to me about this thing called love or what I would come to realize was lust?

Nowadays, when I see fathers and daughters in real life or on television like Randall and Tess on NBC's *This Is Us,* I am a tad jealous because of the communication in their relationship. There's his biological daughter Tess, who expressed to him during Season 3 that she likes girls, and the conversations he has with his adopted daughter Deja, who began dating a young man who is a teenage father. As I watch the dynamics between the father and his daughters, I often wonder how my interest and desires for sex and intimacy would have been shaped, if the adults in my life had more direct conversations with me about the land of ecstasy that I first read about and then began unearthing as a teenager?

During college, a friend and I who were both born to teenage mothers, concluded that our only sex education was founded on one phrase: "Don't bring no baby home." Yet, no one talked with us about boys, babies, or birth control.

"When we were [*sic*] growing up they didn't talk about sex; they didn't talk about mammograms. They didn't talk about anything," said music artist Mary J. Blige during the third episode of the Facebook Watch show *Peace of Mind* with Taraji P. Henson, which focuses on mental health. "We had to find this out on our own; troubleshooting through life."

It wasn't until my 40s that I began discussing matters of love and relationships with my father. "I didn't know you wanted to get married," he said, his words pierced my heart. I was about 45 years old when we had that conversation. In shock, I responded, "You haven't been praying for me; I am unmarried because you haven't been praying," I said angrily before realizing I was basing my desires on the testimonies, I had heard others previously give.

Decades earlier, we had only talked about my dreams of getting married at the beach club his employer allowed company employees to rent. "Daddy make sure you maintain your membership because that's where I want my wedding to be," I would remind him. However, we never talked about who I was dating, how I selected them, what they had to offer, or what I wanted in a future husband. Did he forget the talks about my wedding day and how I wanted to have both my wedding and reception at the facility I fell in love with after attending a wedding there as a teenager?

While I spent time with my father as a child, I didn't grow up thinking I was daddy's little princess. Thus, the dream of being a princess on my wedding day was never a vision I aspired to achieve. As time went on, I realized there were few adult women who had love stories that ended like the fairytales.

Reflection Questions

How did the adults in your life help or harm your understanding of love and relationships?

What do you wish you had known before pursuing your first romantic relationship?

Where are the broken places in your childhood heart that you need God to heal?

Chapter Two

Jesus Is My Boo, Or Maybe Not

———————————— ~~~~ ————————————

How did she do it? She is really saved! I mean, God sure did keep her because I guess she wanted to be kept. Lord, forgive me because I don't know if I wanted to be kept until age 49.

It was a bold and courageous testimony a sister shared during a church's women's conference where she explained that she had remained a virgin after calling her wedding off a few years earlier. It wasn't a discussion I expected given the conference theme; however, it was some sacred information offered during a presentation. Church women are comfortable telling their testimonies of celibacy and abstinence in the walls of the church. Yet, those with different testimonies may not always feel religious settings provide safe spaces to share the role of intimacy or sex in a single woman's life.

On a cold and snowy Sunday, I recall sitting in the pews during praise and worship and sensing a shift in the testimony period. After the female pastor shared while testifying about how long she had been kept, other women began to stand and announce their years of abstinence.

"Don't even look over here," I thought to myself as I joined in the claps of celebration and affirmation. I wasn't actively having sex, but my abstinence calendar couldn't match the testimonies that exceeded a decade.

I don't imagine men would have ever participated in such a testimony service, but women willingly shared how they had been keeping their bodies as a living sacrifice. The girls in the choir are told to keep themselves, while the boys who are musicians are encouraged to sow their holy oats and are given condoms. A man's going to be a man; thus, the same sermonic reminders that "holiness is right," aren't always directed to the brothers who end up in the sheets we spend years holding onto with remorse.

A few years before the morning service with the abstinence roll call, I "accidentally," gave my own Sunday morning testimony while serving as an exhorter, which is a person who transitions a service from praise and worship to the announcements and offering. However, there are no accidents when the Holy Spirit is at work. The spirit was high, as we say when the singing and praying had ushered in the presence of God in a palpable way. As I gave thanks to God for His presence in the service, I felt the tears streaming down my face as I announced; "A few years ago I was driving home after a booty call, (my brain was no longer filtering what was coming out of my mouth), and as I was driving, I fell asleep. Oh, but I woke up because God blocked it. I could have been dead, but God didn't let it be so," I said as others joined in the praise with clapping and shouting.

What did I do? I wondered as I later realized that Sister Simmons hadn't always publicly lived a sanitized life. While one sister gave me an, "I can't believe you did that" eye and nod, another sister came to me later at an afternoon service. "I thank you for this morning. People need to know we're not perfect, and God has brought us from a mighty long way," the then married sister said to me. Although she didn't share her entire story, it was evident her comments were based on that time in history before she was married and had, too, experienced grace and mercy in the area of relationships.

In that moment, I had the audacity to share that God was aware of my "sextivities" and instead of punishment, there was grace. As the saints would say, "I didn't die in my sin" although the Bible says that even innocent babies were born in sin. Unlike the narrative of God striking me down, I received another chance at life and future pleasure.

Years ago, a ministry colleague out of Atlanta started a campaign titled "Celibacy is Sexy," and I was not quite sure what to make of the effort. To me, the word sexy connoted passion, hot, steamy, moist...sex. While I respected his assignment, I'm not sure I'm feeling so sexy about being celibate. Celibacy and abstinence are words, many people often conflate but they're actually different ways of being, although both suggest there are no "sextivities" going down.

Catholic priests and nuns take a vow of celibacy, which means they will abstain from marriage which would lead to sexual relations. Abstinence means that you have voluntarily chosen to refrain from sexual relations.

While sexual abstinence may be easier to maintain as a teen or younger adult, older adults wrestle with refraining from sexual intimacy they have enjoyed for decades. I mean, refraining as a matter of choice and not simply as a matter of circumstance. It's easy to remain abstinent when there are no opportunities, but it's not as easy when there are text messages, social media DMs, and voicemails.

I've been in conferences and revivals where women have been encouraged to pray the desire away, as suggested by male and female preachers. For one associate, those prayers led to a delay in enjoying marital sex. She prayed so hard for her flesh to be suppressed, that it took physical work for the gift of her sensuality to be stirred back up.

I know, there are people who devoutly maintain a lifestyle where they refrain from sexual intimacy. And then there are people who sing in the choir, teach Sunday School, and some even preach as they hide their intimacy and even refrain from public displays of affection.

Although a controversial opinion, I believe it's possible to love God, be unmarried, and also love and desire sexual intimacy. I know, it's blasphemous to many, but it's also a reality that we refuse to acknowledge as women continue to have secret abortions and remain tormented because they haven't embraced a healthy sexuality.

Years ago, when talking with an older mother about my desire for marriage, she leaned in and whispered, "You don't need to get married. I know you got needs," she said, waving her hands to indicate I knew what she was talking about. "Get you a friend and talk to God about that." She wanted me to have another little talk with Jesus. We've been talking for years about my desire to be partnered, legally tangled, sealed by the state, and the Holy Ghost.

I scoffed at the idea, but realized that this woman, who could be my grandmother, knew much more about love and relationships after being in ministry and married for more than fifty years. At that moment, I wondered if she was encouraging me to have agency about my sexuality that women of her day weren't permitted to exert? Or was she saying to me the words she wished someone had said to her?

If only having "a friend" to satisfy my sexual desires were as simple as suggested. Casual sex complicates life, as women are often unable to emotionally detach from their partners because we sometimes desire a deeper relationship while our mouths say, "it's just a little maintenance." True maintenance is being selective about the people we allow into our lives and may choose to explore sexual intimacy with whether as a single person or in marriage.

This discussion may not resonate with some who have chosen to lead a life of abstinence and have never had a, "the Lord saved me after a booty call," testimony to give. I'm glad you haven't had to give that one, as it's not one of my prouder moments. What I am proud of is that I believe that I serve a God who still loves me no matter the offense I may have brought to God or to myself. When God knit me together in my mother's womb, God knew I would have desires for emotional and physical intimacy. If the God I serve is a God of love and reconciliation, then God could handle that confession about a moment God was present in.

Reflection Questions

In what ways have you ever felt guilt or shame about your sexual desires?

In a few words, give yourself permission to articulate your physical desires, (how you want to be touched, how you want to be held, and how you want to be kissed).

How would you describe the intimacy you have experienced with God?

Chapter Three

Lessons From The Lion's Den

I f the adage is true that people come into our lives for reasons, seasons, or lifetimes, I've learned that some people come into our lives to teach us lessons we didn't know we needed to learn. They bring us assignments we would have missed had they not been posted in life's syllabus.

In 2001, I was 27 years old and fresh out of graduate school when I moved to Charlotte, North Carolina, to begin my career as a college instructor. But when it came to my love life, I quickly became the student who needed more hours to graduate after clearly failing all of her remedial courses on romantic relationships. Although I went to college 20 minutes away from Charlotte, there was something different about living in the Queen City as a grown bill-paying woman with her own dwelling place. Weeks before starting my teaching job, I took a job at a call center where I met a Liberian man who was dressed as if he was a model for Polo or Hilfiger. We met one day during a break, and his swagger and accent quickly drew me in as his eyes scanned my young voluptuous body. His father was a college professor, so he had grown up with some privilege and had this high-pitched laugh. He was fine to me, and his kisses were always sweet. However, he had more stories than I had time to read. We started hanging out consistently until one Saturday morning when I called his home phone number.

I'm still not sure whether it was a wife, girlfriend, baby mama, or sister from another mister who answered the phone, "Who dis?" before beginning a loud exchange in a tongue I couldn't interpret. "Ummmmm, ummmm, let me call you back, dear," he said before hanging up the telephone. He arrived later with an apology and more sweet kisses. But that ship had sailed because it was more drama than I could manage.

During this time, I started praying more intentionally for a husband, but apparently, God had me in the queue: *Please hold for the next available bachelor.* Up until this time, I had only dated American-born men, but Charlotte allowed me access to experience love from beyond the borders. Weeks after asking my Liberian sweet-kisser to stop calling, I met the "Bajan Lion."

I was a new college instructor on a break between classes when I met him at a Chinese restaurant in the University area of Charlotte. He, too, had recently relocated to the area, when the investment company he worked for moved a major part of their operations South. It was his West Indian accent that mirrored my Gullah Geechee tongue that did it for me. Although I sensed he was much older, he had the sculpted body of a 20-year-old. I could see it through his shirt that bore his work badge. "He got benefits," is how we often translate work badges even when we can't read the wearer's government name.

I was shocked when this gorgeous specimen of a man initiated keeping in touch beyond this lunch break. I felt attractive but didn't think I was attractive enough to attract a man like this. I know I'm not alone in that thought. Not everyone walks around thinking they're the "Baddest Bish." A few days later, we met for lunch and then dinner and then... the rest is a tale of passion and tangling. If there was ever such a thing as an entanglement, it is what we had.

During our time together, we grieved singer Aaliyah's death by cooking dinner and listening to Power 98 FM, navigated the events of September 11 together, and cuddled up in a blanket listening to B.B.

King weeks after the 911 events that impacted many of his family and friends. He read lots of ancient Eastern philosophy, so he often had these dense interpretations of things. It was during those conversations that I was trying to make sense of his spirituality; those talks established the intimacy I most desired.

Our connection was fueled by our love of culture and spontaneity. Unlike other "situationships" I had before, we actively dated, cooked dinner together, and laughed. He always derailed my plans and canceled my, "Be strong, Arlecia" talks I'd have with myself before spending time with him. Let's just say one morning I woke up with my panty girdle securing my locs since I never made it home.

He taught me a freedom I had never known, as well as an appreciation for the gift of our bodies. We talked a lot about our bodies, and he even shared this tragic story about how he had to help a former lover with her personal care. "What? Get out of here." He sucked his teeth and then proceeded to tell me that she was a professional woman who didn't know how to properly wash her vagina. "Yeah, man. She was washing the surface. I had to show her how to take her rag and get inside of there. She was a beautiful woman, but I couldn't believe she was walking around with an odor because she didn't know how to wash her coochie."

Oh, wow! The conversation was actually sparked one day when he complimented me on my hygiene. That's a conversation I've had more than once with men who felt comfortable talking about women, they had been with, who didn't practice good hygiene. Based on some of the conversations I've had with women who were told things like they couldn't take showers during their cycles and other folk wisdom didn't yield the cleanest of "pocketbooks," as my granny would call a woman's private area. While no one had told me how to use my pocketbook, there was an early charge to always wash the pocketbook.

The Lion trained in various martial arts and loved his body, which means he would walk around the house naked. No shirt, no underwear, just butt naked. Of course, I wasn't that secure, and we talked about those body issues I had. "You're beautiful, but you're too young to carry so much weight," he would say. I later appreciated that he was not afraid to confront me about my weight although I was initially offended. Of course, I rolled my neck and said, "You didn't say that last night," knowing full well he was telling the truth. I was 4'11 and I weighed more than 200 pounds.

My weight was an issue, but then it wasn't an issue. It was the first time I had experienced PDA (personal displays of affection), and I acted as if I hated him licking on my neck in the grocery store while secretly, I felt validated by his squeezes as I selected salad dressing. One night, we went to the movies and as we exited out, I remember seeing a group of attractive and thinner women. I'm guessing he sensed my insecurity and pulled me closer as we went to the car. It's that affirming PDA that we often reject that honestly, we desire but sometimes never receive.

As I savored the lovin' I received, I soon learned I was on borrowed time. I was technically involved in an entanglement without my knowledge. My intentions were always to go home when I visited him, so I never had a "spinnanight bag." One night when he went to take a shower, I went to the linen closet so I could use the other bathroom. But there was something not quite right about the towels I discovered. I mean, these towels had eyelet trim and screamed, "Sis, a woman bought me!" or "Chile, I was requested on the wedding registry." For weeks, he tried to convince me that he was the proud owner of the

Patti LaBelle cookbook on the kitchen counter.

After probing him about all of the various feminine items in his home, he finally admitted he had a girlfriend that he left in New York. Her household goods had been shipped along with his during the corporate move. She was looking for a position in Charlotte and had scheduled interviews. She was on her way to be with her man. Meanwhile, I'm sitting there looking like "Boo-Boo the Fool," planning his 40th birthday party in my head. I'm trying to think through a budget and how I could get the one friend he had in the area to gather people. By the time November came, his girlfriend would be the one hosting anything concerning him.

The only option he could offer me was for us to remain in a "situationship," while he played house in the apartment we had christened. "I mean, you have your own place and she'll be over there," he said as if it made perfect sense. That morning as he drove me home, I couldn't believe he had "fixed his mouth" to suggest such a thing. As we got closer to my gated apartment complex, I felt a sharp pain in my chest. "Is this what heartbreak feels like," I asked myself as I reconciled that this was the end of what I considered my good thing. He walked me to the door and kissed me goodbye.

The Lion wasn't perfect, and I had challenged him about the role he was not playing in his son's life, but he permitted me to dig for intimacy in a way that I never envisioned. Even if one of the issues that simmered in the background was, we weren't "equally yoked" when it came to our faith.

His relationship with God or lack thereof, was problematic for me. He was "spiritual" while I was religious. I was a cradle-Baptist who was challenging her childhood theology while he had abandoned the faith of his childhood.

During our time together, my relationship with God was strengthening and I started faithfully attending a Church of God in Christ Church where every week I was reminded of how holiness was right. I would lift his name during prayers, and ask God to block or confirm what I was involved in. The church and denomination's articulation of holiness did not make room for the intimacy I shared in the Lion's Den. When I learned more about glossolalia, or speaking in tongues, I wrestled with how this same mouth could speak mysteries and perform oral sex. (If you are married, I trust you have learned how to multitask.)

I'm not sure it would have been so easy to walk away if there wasn't another woman involved. Weeks later, I deemed my departure from the Lion's Den as God's way of escape. I had escaped the fire of lust. Holiness was right, and the holiness I was learning about required that I "keep myself," which I did for three years after my time with the Lion.

However, the Lion's work in my life wasn't completely done. I had taken his advice, and I began walking around my apartment complex before I went to work. I also changed what I ate and how I cooked. Before long, the weight started dropping. A month or so later, I was getting dressed when I heard the doorbell. It was the Lion wearing a pair of sweatpants that made you take notice and say, "That right there is something the Lord made."

"Stay focused, Arlecia," I recalled saying to myself. "Fix your mind on Jesus!"

He had trailed a car through the gate. I stood at the door in a bathrobe and stood guard over my heart. He was not coming into my house or back into my life. "I can tell you're losing weight," he said. "I'm doing a little something, something." By this time on the journey, I didn't desire to be with him physically. I was on my way to Bible study.

His girlfriend finally arrived in Charlotte, and we stopped communicating.

The next year, I relocated back to South Carolina for my second teaching job. Years later, we tried to reconnect one weekend when he came to visit my rural town. Sadly, something didn't gel and the fun we had previously shared in Charlotte couldn't be replicated. The fire sparked on that hot summer day couldn't be reignited.

Reflection Questions

Was there ever a time where you negotiated what you honestly wanted in a relationship while being offered only a portion of what you desired? If so, how did you feel after settling for less than you deserved?

Think back to a failed romantic relationship in your past. What did that individual come to teach you?

In what ways has God blocked or disrupted relationships you now realize you were never assigned to be in?

Chapter Four

Sorry, J.Lo, My Love Does Cost A Thing

My teenage dad was not a deadbeat; however, our relationship was complicated.

He took me on vacations, cooked me dinner at his bachelor pad, took me out for meals, and made sure I got to know his side of the family. As a teenager, we once went to eat lunch at this historic hotel in downtown Charleston. He spotted some female friends in the restaurant and was shocked when they were hesitant to greet him. Later, one of the women shared that she thought he was with his girlfriend, so she avoided eye contact and didn't speak to him. My dad is only 17 years my senior, so there was often outward confusion about our relationship. He and my little brother visited me during my freshman year of college, he popped his collar when he sensed a dorm hallmate was checking him out. By today's standards, he would be a "Zaddy," an attractive older man who appeals to younger women. He's funny, is always well dressed, and he's been easy on many eyes over the years.

One of the most memorable activities I recall is shopping trips during Christmas or the start of school once I became a teenager. One year, he took me to a store called Thalhimers where he allowed me to select a few outfits and a boombox. Yep, a boombox that I kept until I was age 26 when the old school electronic finally gave up the ghost. I always had nice clothes, but this shopping experience was something different. My mother, a savvy budget shopper and the queen of layaway was a tad perplexed by the costly adventure but later realized how much that day meant to me. What my father spent on only a few items, she would have gotten in a few Christmas gifts, too.

My 13-year-old self loved to dance to Gwen Guthrie's "Ain't Nothin Goin' on But the Rent," where she passionately told her partner that he needed a job. It wasn't a new theory when the song was released, as some women have grown up hearing about the expectations of men who wanted their time or affection. While some were shocked when Cardi B and Megan Thee Stallion rapped about the power of the WAP, black grandmamas had long told daughters and granddaughters that no one with WAP should have unpaid bills or unmet needs. It's that mother's wit we don't publicly talk about that often leads to derailing girls at an early age. Honestly, I hadn't engaged in such conversations until I reached adulthood, but many friends have shared this communal wisdom that was passed down to them.

In my 30s, I wondered how such activities shaped who I became. Because my father was married with three more children, I didn't spend as much time with him as I desired. I realized those trips represented being loved. As I grew older, went to college, and became a working adult, I finally realized that our relationship had become transactional. When I assessed why I interacted with men the way I did and came with the expectations they didn't often meet, I realized I had interpreted my father's love through presents and not presence.

When I began dating in my 20s, I had this strange thing going on where I always wanted men to buy me something. "Did you get me something for my birthday?" I would ask. As of this writing, I haven't found one of those bill-paying men some women brag about dating even as I desired to be with someone who could buy me gifts.

When I assessed my expectations that weren't met, I realized that this desire could have gotten me into a harmful relationship had the wrong man learned of this weakness. The need for this kind of validation has landed women in abusive relationships and prostitution. I don't recall the moment, but I'm glad I finally acknowledged that no amount of gifts bought by a man's hands would provide the authentic love and intimacy I sought.

Not only did this "transactional love" cause me to desire gifts, it influenced how I decided to express my interest or attempted to secure affection. I didn't know anything about "love languages" back then, but even if I did, my actions were not consistent with what I desired.

I was a teenager when I began buying gifts for men. I remember buying a guy in high school a shirt because I wanted him to like me. I threw it out the window of the school bus as he walked to his bus. In college, I recall dragging my soror Shana, through multiple stores in the Galleria Mall in Rock Hill, South Carolina, so I could buy a guy I had just met at the club a birthday gift. We went out days after his birthday, and I wanted to show him how much I liked him. I didn't buy him one gift, but I ordered him a monogrammed turtleneck since he is a December baby.

Did you read that I had just met him once and had talked on the phone with him only a few times, yet I was willing to spend my college job money on gifts? Shana thought I was crazy, although the self-diagnosis hadn't come yet. We're still friends to this day, and I later realized he had no neck for a turtleneck.

The crazier thing is, I was willing to spend money on others that I wouldn't even spend on myself.

I started 2020 getting to know a man from my hometown. While we had no plans for

Valentine's Day, I planned on giving him something he could use for a future venture. Since he had expressed an interest in cooking and establishing himself as a food vendor, I wanted to get him something to support his dream. After I combined a couple of coupons, I was able to get him a 10-piece Biltmore stainless steel knife set that was originally priced at $225.

While we saw each other earlier in the week, our weekend plans didn't pan out and I ended up never giving him the gift. Ironically, we had talked every day that week except on Valentine's Day when he didn't even call. Surprisingly, the no-neck recipient of the turtleneck purchased 25 years earlier sent me roses to my office. For months, the knives sat in my closet as I debated returning them or giving them away to someone else.

One day, I sat back and realized that these knives represented a pattern I thought I had earlier disrupted. However, I was turning that corner again: equating gifts with love. He never asked for a gift, but I was giving him something I wanted to give him because down inside I had the ulterior motive or agenda of convincing him that I was worth his love and time. When he didn't buy his mother a gift by the day of her birthday, I felt some kind of way and hoped this wasn't a sign of what was not to come. As the coronavirus pandemic raged on and things began to shut down, things came to a screeching halt as our communication became rocky. The final nail in the proverbial coffin was when he told me he couldn't come to see me because he didn't have anyone to keep his dog. But that's another story for another book.

It may be an unwarranted credit charge for some people, while for others, it has been exchanging sex, housing, the use of a vehicle, credit, and other material goods. Somewhere along the road, we learned that if I like you, I should give you things with the expectation that you will reciprocate in the way I desire. And if you like or love me, you should do the same.

In the end, the desperation of diggin' for intimacy leaves many with a financial deficit and emotionally bankrupt.

Reflection Questions

In what ways have you ever tried to buy your way into someone's heart?

In what ways have you exchanged your affection, body, or time for goods or services?

How has God helped you recognize your worth beyond credentials, relationships, success, and material possessions?

Chapter Five

The Secrets of the Sheets

---~~---

In pop culture such as movies and television shows, there are often references to a man's, "Little Black Book." When a character gets married or begins dating seriously, he must determine whether he will throw out the book filled with contacts of past conquests in order to commit to the new relationship and break old ties. These days, the connections are stored digitally in mobile phones and Google contacts.

When relationships end, people get blocked and unfriended on social media. But no matter how many ways we try to disconnect from communicating with them, the people we have allowed to enter our spirits can never be forgotten. You may not call them, but anytime their favorite sports team plays, you think about that time you spent time with them tailgating. A whiff of a former lover's favorite cologne an aisle over in the grocery store often catches your attention as you try to confirm it's not him. Women connect with their lovers in ways that have us thinking about them long after whatever connections we had. Meanwhile, brothers can move on to the next situation without the emotional connections.

Did you know that it's possible for a man to have sex with you and then forget your name? Yes, not only is it possible but it happened to me in 2012. Yes, the good doctor had just finished having lunch with her family members in one of her favorite Charleston restaurants. I was waiting for a relative who was using the restroom and I noticed a man whose face looked familiar. I had noticed the group of people earlier, but I was now up close and saw his face. He was waiting for members of his dining party, but when I saw him, I said, "Excuse me, did you work for a computer company or something?"

"Yes," he responded. At that moment, I remembered his name. "Is your name C?" "Yes," I smiled and realized he didn't know me from Adam's cat or however that euphemism goes. Perplexed he replies, "What's your name?" "It's Arlecia," I said with a look of, "Don't bother trying to remember, you don't. You don't remember me."

That bastard didn't remember me. Sorry for the expletive, but that is what I would have said if I had the chance to publicly lament. I said nothing and prayed my relatives who were nearby did not follow-up on the discussion. How embarrassing. How berating. I hadn't seen him in about 12 years and at that time he remembered me and we shared greetings. Yet this time he didn't know my face. My face. The face that had looked in his face as we did what only the Lord knows, and what only his neighbors could hear, some 19 years ago. I don't care if it was 19 years ago, he should have remembered my name.

The woman I had seen him with on this day was likely the same woman he was with a few years ago when I saw him in the big girl's store where I worked part-time. He appeared to be married and looked settled and happy, but he did not know my name. And why would he? I had given him the inner parts of me in exchange for a few phone calls, dinner, a movie, and the promise of a future. But there would be no future and not even the memory of my name.

I met him one summer while I was working at the hospital and he came to fix our photocopier. I mentioned that I was interested in him to one of the seasoned workers, and by his second visit to the office we had exchanged phone numbers. One call led to a dinner and a movie date, which led to the reason I believe he should have remembered my name for the rest of his life. Details are sketchy about why our little tryst never developed into more, but I recall I was in college and he was a working man who had a girlfriend who had just moved out of his apartment. Well, maybe. I do recall investigating and noticing that some of her things were still in his apartment behind a door I wasn't supposed to open. I'm telling you, it's amazing what we find in drawers, closets, and behind doors, we're not supposed to open, while visiting people we are dating, getting to know, or whatever situation is developing.

Why? Why? Why?

Why ladies do we settle for this kind of behavior? Why do we reduce ourselves to sharing sheets with men who are already in relationships? Men who will one day forget our names? That incident of not being properly identified went straight to the marrow. And once again, my little sanctified and set apart self, was reminded that I had a past of secret sheets.

My twenty-something season of searching for love and what looked like security, (a car, a job, and one's own apartment), often looks like a jackpot to women in their late teens and possibly even in their late 60s, as women like my younger self are in search of someone or something to satisfy unmet needs. In some cases, it's a search for the little girl who lacked protection or security in childhood to seek it through a partner who is not fully equipped to address the emotional needs that are often equated to material ones.

He was not a bad guy, but he was a grown man who had already lived with a woman and I was a college student wanting more than he was willing to extend. I am guessing the man I saw on this day is not the first, nor will he be the last, who has not remembered my name. Heck, there are some whom I have shared sheets with, and I don't recall their names, addresses, or even their eyes. *Just clutch your pearls and keep reading.*

While I was working in rural South Carolina as a news reporter, I once talked with a woman who tried helping a young woman secure governmental assistance and she noted she asked for the father's social security number. The middle-aged divorced woman said, and I have forever remembered it, "You don't ask a man his social security number before you have sex."

No, we don't ask for that nor do some of us ask for their full names, real ages, or marital status. If he appears to want us, love us, or will spend time with us, then we can get all of those small details at a later time. That is if there is a later time and not a one-night or -day stand.

Beloved, I shared this story because on that day I experienced a degree of guilt and pain that I had not experienced in some time.

Well, I take that back. As I was writing, I recalled that this was the same restaurant where months earlier I had spotted another man's ex-wife and family. Years earlier, the woman had learned of my name from e-mails exchanged between me and her then-husband. Yes, another shameful sheet moment. I wrote about that indiscretion in a digital article published by *The Root* on February 4, 2014.

While it was ironic that both incidents occurred in the same restaurant, what was also ironic is that this restaurant sits on the bank of the Ashley River in Charleston and is located appropriately three miles from the Charleston Slave Market. The river would have been a site where people once kneeled to clean their physical bodies, clothes, and to be baptized to cleanse their spirits. Although soiled and tattered sheets may linger in our lives, I am grateful for grace and God's cleansing power to restore us even when we're all tangled in secret sheets.

Reflection Questions

During memorial services, we speak the name and acknowledge the absence of those who have transitioned from life to death. Although people may physically still be alive, our relationships with them may have died. Whose names must you speak to release them from your "sheets" and your soul?

If given an opportunity for a peaceful encounter, what would you say to someone who has wounded you or didn't acknowledge the intimacy shared?

Who do you need God to help you forgive? Who do you need to request forgiveness from due to your actions in a past relationship?

Chapter Soix

What Ha Happened Was...

---~---

After answering my call to ministry at the age of 36, I began to receive more and more invitations to minister to girls and women in a variety of settings. Before writing my first book *Diggin' For Treasure: Jewels of Hope When Pressure and Time Collide* my preaching and teaching rarely provided me the opportunity to discuss sexuality in religious spaces. From time-to-time, I could reference it in presentations, but a deep dive into how women have found themselves in the relationship ruts we end up in didn't fit well into the conferences focused on Ruth and Boaz. I mean, Ruth did have somewhat of a situationship we could all identify with, although her connection at the threshing floor resulted in marriage.

As a young woman, I enjoyed coming home from college and going out to nightclubs with my girlfriends from high school. I looked forward to these Friday and Saturday nights where we would seek out, "Ladies Free before 11 p.m.," deals so we could go and check out the scene. We weren't big drinkers, and my friends weren't big on dancing, but we enjoyed these hours of checking out the latest spots in our hometown, "The Holy City."

In addition to getting in free and 10 cents wing specials, I was often hoping I would catch someone's attention. You know, make eye contact, or get a guy to give me the "What's up?" head tilt. I wanted something to be up. I wanted him to come over, ask me to dance, and then request my phone number for a date. Whether you are 20 or 50, there is the desire to get that "What's up?"

Why was the need for that "What's up" so valuable to me, and why did I feel the need to secure it from a man? Those are the kinds of questions I wish I had a chance to explore prior to adulthood. These are the types of questions I envisioned my ministry would entail as I journeyed alongside other women whom I prayed with not having similar experiences. Take, for example, a group of teen girls I had a chance to meet with during a youth event at a Baptist Church, where I was supposed to talk with the girls about "being a queen" or something of that nature.

Of course, I went with my notes about how to be a Proverbs 31 woman, with the hopes of exploring how to be a virtuous woman. But then God had another plan. During the period given to chat with the young ladies, God had them ask some of the toughest questions I had ever encountered about sex and sexuality. One had questions about why their mother could overlook their father having an affair and didn't cuss the women out when she called their house.

"Well, adulthood is complicated," I began as I stumbled through responding to the question. "I'm sure your mother doesn't like what is happening, and she's making whatever decisions she's making with you and your siblings in mind. Don't disrespect her; pray for and with her. She is confronted with some difficult choices. You don't understand it, but it's something that only she and your dad can address."

This teenager was not trying to hear the excuses I was attempting to make for her mother who was a devoted church member and mother. There was pain in her eyes, a pain I had known before as a daughter who also questioned how her own mother interacted with the men in her life. I understood this frustration as a teen girl who once questioned if the relational choices, she had watched her mother make were the best for her or even her mother.

I was so uncomfortable having this discussion, but I knew it was a discussion that they needed to have. They didn't want to hear about a virtuous woman in antiquity that they couldn't see themselves in; rather, they wanted to know how to deal with challenges they were seeing in living color.

Another high schooler asked, "Am I still a virgin if someone did something to me when I was five?" I needed the Father, Son, and Holy Ghost to help me give a response that affirmed this young woman's humanity, reinforce that sex was good and of God, and leave her and the others with a suitable reply. "You're not damaged property; God knows you didn't make that decision at 5 years old."

I did the best to answer that question, and since that evening, I have tried to ask God for the answers that would help affirm other women whose first sexual encounter was not of their choosing. The session lasted longer than the church had allotted, but I was grateful that the youth leaders didn't interrupt the moment. That night, I prayed over each of them as they tightly gripped hands and leaned on one another when the pain was too overwhelming. While I likely needed another adult in the room to support them and spiritually support me as the Spirit was moving, I am forever grateful for the Holy Spirit had made intercession. The strength we all needed was a very present help.

When the young women left out of the room hugging one another and with tears in their eyes, I'll never forget hearing an adult scream down the hall, "Well, what's wrong?" God had met us, healed us, and provided the space where the wounds they had experienced could be treated, instead of bandaged and hidden. For far too long, church leaders have muted discussions on violations possibly out of fear they would have to confront congregants or report them to the authorities. Either way, our sacred spaces haven't always been a place where we could lay all of our burdens down.

I left that night wondering what if similar spaces could be provided to younger and older women where they could dig for answers that helped them better understand issues of intimacy and sexuality. Real talk, the girl grieved by the relationship she saw her mother having with her father who was allegedly cheating, will take those wounds into her future intimate relationships. Just imagine if in adolescence we could have gotten a head start on our trust issues that later developed?

In a different setting, I hosted a wellness camp for children ages 8-14. We started each day with spiritual meditation, cultural enrichment, and physical health were among the programming topics. Thankfully, the pastor I worked with approved the session and allowed me to invite in a female clinical psychologist, who was also a minister, to talk about "Good touch, bad touch." The title was one I picked up from another church while I was traveling as an evangelist.

All of the parents signed waivers so their children could participate, and I chose to sit outside of the two sessions so the children could feel comfortable expressing themselves to the therapist. Thankfully, the therapist didn't have to file any reports about any abuse detected after the two sessions where she used puppets to discuss anatomy. The puppets weren't needed, as the children knew more than we expected.

Reflection Questions

Thinking back to your childhood, what are questions you had about love, relationships, or sex that were never addressed until adulthood?

Take a few minutes and write a one-page letter to your 13-year-old self about what you wanted to know about love, relationships, or sex. If you do not recall having thoughts on those areas at that age, consider a letter to your 21-year-old self.

How do you believe God can use you to help prepare children in your family or community for adulthood?

Chapter 7

Don't Scroll To Your Death: Online Dating

My youngest aunt is only nine years older, so I have vivid memories of interrogations that took place when she began dating.

"Well, who are your people? Where are your mama people from?" My grandmother would ask question after question while my grandfather was likely outside taking down the brother's license plate. Most were too afraid to catch the bus or walk in our hood.

Trust, people from church and community were contacted for additional information. While I always thought these questions were intrusive, I later realized mama was just trying to make sure her child was safe. My own father has said about my maternal grandmother, "Weese didn't play." If only some of us asked more of the same questions and didn't play when it came to our safety.

Between the show *Catfish* and other incidents, we hear about from associates and friends, I am beginning to wonder whether we ask enough questions. As dating adults, many of us fail to ask pertinent questions. (I know some people believe in courting and that is a different post for a different date). We will plan a trip requiring our passports, yet we won't even know our companion's full legal name unless the document falls on the floor.

When I worked as a reporter in a rural town, I frequented a resource center where residents accessed various support services. One day, the director was assisting a young woman who needed assistance to care for her newborn. During one of our many off-the-record conversations, the director explained the woman could not access some services without the father's social security number. "Nobody gets a social security number before they screw," she angrily said as we stood in the parking lot. It was tight, but it was right.

I admit to secretly retrieving and reviewing a driver's license or two. Hey, God takes care of babies, fools, and bootleg private investigators. We trust a nice beard and a smile and invite people into our personal spaces without intimately getting to know them before sharing our bodies and vital information. Television shows like TV One's *Fatal Attraction* and *Snapped* are constant reminders that you can spend years with a person and not really know them.

In September 2017, I was numb after reading a news report about 35-year-old Jeannine Shante Skinner's stabbing death. The college professor was found dead in her apartment, and police immediately suspected Skinner's boyfriend, who had days before taken a picture with her while attending church. As a college professor who had previously worked at the same university as Skinner, the story resonated with me and prompted me to write a reflection piece published by *ForHarriet.com*. In April 2018, her 45-year-old boyfriend plead guilty to second-degree murder. WCNC Charlotte reported the boyfriend's mental illness was cited in the plea deal. Skinner was stabbed more than 200 times.

Although we can't live life in the Witness Protection Program, unless you are in cahoots with "the gubment," we can pray for discernment. As you mix and mingle, ask God to let you hear what is not being spoken by human lips and see what may not be visible. When it doesn't feel right, consider it not right. Let that not-so-good feeling be well with your soul!

If you don't feel right about a new acquaintance stopping by your house, then invite them to meet you for coffee or a milkshake at Sonic. Just swirl the straw if nothing else. I know what is being advised sounds elementary at best, but we must guard not only our hearts but also our lives.

Reflection Questions

What information about a partner have you ignored because it would end the relationship?

What would you do if you thought a relationship was placing you in emotional, financial, or physical danger?

Thinking back, how has God helped you discern that a relationship was harmful or toxic?

Chapter 8
The Soundtrack of Heartbreak

The year I was born, Minnie Riperton sang a love song that left lovers thinking birds were singing directly to them. When she died at the age of 31, in the summer of 1979, I was a five-year-old captivated by the melody used to describe a state I never imagined would later be so complicated. If only love was as melodic, radiant, and unblemished as Riperton's voice interpreted it to be.

In less than 10 years after that night where the adults played her songs loudly as they mourned her death, I would learn that love and relationships wouldn't always leave my heart with a "La-la-la-la-la." Oh, some good lovemaking will have you singing a new song, but so often we find ourselves singing tunes of lament.

By now you've realized the impact music has had in shaping my framework of intimacy. As a 13-year-old, one of my favorite songs was, "Love Overboard" by Gladys Knight & The Pips. Yes, rap music was on the scene, but I grew up in a home where Natalie Cole, Luther Vandross, Ashford & Simpson, and Deniece Williams were in daily rotation. I would soon begin developing my list of favorite love songs watching Donnie Simpson on BET's *Video Soul* or listening to the black-owned WPAL Radio Station or Z93. Although the song was penned more than 30 years ago, the lyrics are still relevant as girlfriends continue the diatribe. I didn't know what kind of love Ms. Gladys was talking about, but that love penned by Midnight Star member Reginald Calloway's hand was serious.

Galloway, who penned songs for Teddy

Pendergrass and Levert, wrote about a love worth holding on to, which was likened to one going overboard on a ship. That was some serious love. Ms. Gladys sang she was running out of time and about to lose her mind! Honey, that was something serious there.

Little did I know, the behaviors and emotions expressed in the love or love-gone-wrong songs would become lived experiences as I navigated puberty. From artists like Keith Sweat who provided the soundtrack when I lost my virginity to artists Mary J. Blige who later provided more tracks that expressed the conditions of the heart.

As a teenager, I heard discussions about protecting our ear gates. Back then some of the rationale and theology appeared fuzzy, but it wasn't until I became an adult that I understood more about how conversations and religious teachings on why some genres of music needed to be avoided or selected carefully because of the impact the lyrics could have on your life.

I mean, my musical sensibilities were at their height when a male writer who will remain unnamed, wrote about how a woman reminded him of a Jeep while others had me waiting in anticipation for someone to think of me day and night because they couldn't get me off of their mind. What if we wrote new songs where healing and restoration were at the forefront of the lyrics? Songs, where the totality of who we were, was lyrically expressed. What if instead of learning about sensuality from lyrics that promoting licking and sucking, there were spaces where we could have discussed what really happens during sex?

Why do our bodies feel the way they do when they are caressed, touched, or licked? Why are we physically attracted to people whose souls are cold?
Why are we attracted to the scents of

others?

How does all of that connect to creating a whole human?

Was there a manual or book someone could have provided beyond album liner notes? As an inquisitive child, I found a way to read about any and everything I wanted to know about. I'll never recall being in the seventh grade and reading a book titled *Menstruation* on the school bus.

I didn't see anything unusual about reading about this process until an eighth-grader named Monique says, "Arlecia, hold that book up." A grade older, she couldn't believe that I had no shame in learning more about my body.

I've often been both shocked and saddened in conversations with other women who had limited knowledge about how their bodies functioned. While music had the physical act covered, there's so much misinformation and lack of information that I could spend hundreds of pages talking about the unknown. And just because a woman is seasoned, doesn't mean she's knowledgeable about sensuality and sex. For example, a few years ago, I ventured out with a clergy sister to a remixed Maundy Thursday service where she was responsible for facilitating one of the activities for a program that was much different than anything I had experienced before. People who had been married for decades gained new insight as my friend discussed love languages and guided members of the mostly elderly congregation through a deeper understanding of Jesus washing the disciples' feet on the night in which he was betrayed.

That night, we passed around crudites and washed each other's hands instead of feet to accommodate the older congregants. There were Aha-moments for many as many who were married longer than we were alive realized in the words of Anthony Hamilton, "the point of it all."

"Now I know why he's always touching me and wants to be touched," said the bride of 61 years.

It was in a church's fellowship where no music was played that a woman learned how to re-imagine expressing love to her mate.

Reflection Questions

While *"Jesus Loves The Little Children"* may have been one of the first songs some learned, what are some of the songs that make you think more deeply about love, romance, and sexuality?

Write lyrics you would include in a song about the love you currently have or desire to have one day?

What are the songs that sustain and remind you of God's love?

Chapter 9

Reclaiming My Time

─────────────⌒─────────────

When you're diggin' for intimacy through companionship, it's easy to put your guard down and become prey to dating candidates who wouldn't make the cut if you observed a more thorough vetting process.

One of the lessons I learned as a result of an entanglement is you should always stick with what you know. In my 20s and 30s, I used my journalistic research skills to always learn more about any suitors before they could willingly provide information. Before there was anything such as a Google search, there were friends who worked at the insurance company or other agencies where background information could be accessed. No, I wasn't trying to check their credit score, but I did want to know if there were any plea bargains for alleged homicides, domestic violence cases, or anything else that would indicate I WAS IN HARM'S way.

Whether you are 22 or 62 we all come to the table with past experiences, knowledge, trouble, indiscretions, and things that we like to keep between us and Jesus. When I turned 40, I noticed I began letting my guard down and stopped being nosey. I stopped my nonstop inquiries, although some say I still asked too many questions, and I surrendered to just allow for myself to organically get to know someone. Instead of doing an extensive background check on individuals, I would begin to see people as clean slates allowing them to write their stories right in front of my eye. Oh, but we all know there's no such thing as a blank slate.

Well, while it sounded like a good idea and would be less intrusive, I learned in 2016 that the vetting protocols I had used in the past actually worked. As I approached my first official vacation as a pastor, I met a tall drank of sweet tea with agave while running errands after a hair appointment. I was getting ready to fly out for some fun in the sun in New Orleans, where I would get the chance to spend time with a platonic friend who lived in the region.

Tall and dark with that nice salt and pepper beard standing in the parking lot getting all in my business about why I am in my car minding my business. We went back and forth making conversation, and then he pulled out his lil flip phone and asked for my phone number. I should have known something when he pulled out his "Obama phone" in 2016. No grown man under the age of 70-years-old with viable employment is walking around with a flip phone. But he was cute, and I was hot, and he asked me for my number.

My head was so in the clouds as I prepared to be away for almost a week that I actually forgot his name. I wasn't talking to anyone, so I knew his voice when he first called. It's not like me to not get a name and the complete spelling for further investigation, but I was single ready to mingle as well as hot and bothered. Hot being the greater of the duo.

But I should have run after the first meeting that would follow a few days later. When he arrived dressed in a short pants leisure suit laced with the name of a fictitious sports team, possibly something that came from Maxway (Hey, I'm not hating on Maxway; their summer dresses are bae)! He explained that he was rushing to meet me on time, so he left his wallet.

He told me this before we got into the restaurant, so there was time to run. There was a mall nearby, so he suggested we just go and walk in the mall. Because I had been waiting for this meal most of the day, I offered to treat him to dinner since I came to eat. The outfit alone should have made me run, but he was fine, and as granny would say, "I was hot in the pants." We sat down, he had hot wings and fries, and the rest was a sordid hot mess of history that lasted for about four months.

You haven't found yourself in a "good entanglement" until you say to God, a best friend, and your mama: "If the Lawd gets me out of this; then I won't ever do this again." Between the lies about who he was, a woman calling me directly and threatening to call my church, and everything else he legally had attached to him, I had let my guard down and had sashayed into a summer fling with a man who had previously been sent to jail for not registering as a sex offender. Although he was not physically abusive, he was manipulative, siphoned money out of me, and even required that I pay him and another guy for moving me across town.

"Arlecia, how in the ENTIRE HELL did you end up here?" I often asked myself. I knew how: I was in a new city alone, pastoring a church filled with challenges, and he provided companionship. That is when he could leave the woman, he lived with a few miles away, wasn't daydreaming about winning the lottery, or convincing me he was such an asset to his church family. He was unemployed as a result of his legal issues and allegedly a work-related accident, so he was available. I paid for that availability in more ways than one.

Between behavioral responses, I had seen when I confronted him about his lies, and the actual stories that always had some kind of cliffhanger, I'm not sure which issues he had that may have been in the DSM-5, a diagnostic tool used by mental health professionals. There were so many stories to dissect that I needed the connections and investigative powers of Olivia Pope to decipher fact from fiction. One day, I mustered up the courage to start back at step one and Google his name. I found his most recent court records, which were consistent with the legal issues he had previously told me about.

During that time, I had made the first call to the ecclesial leadership of the denomination I served and alerted them that I thought I needed to resign after returning from vacation. Although I was encouraged to stay and begin a pastoral coaching program, the crisis in my professional and spiritual life, snuffed out the discernment I needed that would have had me running for the hills sooner rather than later. In my desperation for support and a physical presence in my life, I attracted a lover who did more emotional harm than good.

Whether he had a diagnosable condition or not, I ended the "situationship" realizing I needed some psychological counseling. I will admit, I was in the midst of a crisis, so I attracted a walking, living, breathing trauma situation. And according to Queen Mother Iyanla Vanzant in a YouTube video teaching, "All relationships are a reflection of ourselves."

Reflection Questions

How have you sacrificed your peace or even your health for the sake of companionship?

Recall a time when you ignored the red flags in a relationship. What were the greatest lessons learned from that experience?

Write a short prayer for yourself or a friend who is unable to become untangled, don't know they're tangled, or desire to be free from relationships that have diminished their self-esteem, finances, and status in life.

Chapter 10

Resting My Field

O ur bodies, minds, and even our vaginas can heal after they have rested.

"There is a time for everything, and a season for every activity under the heavens:"

Ecclesiastes 3:1

When I journeyed to Iowa City, Iowa, to attend graduate school, I learned the most that I ever wanted or needed to know about farming. Iowa is known for its corn crops, while some confuse it with Idaho, known for potatoes. I experienced severe weather conditions, from a historical flood that saturated the earth for weeks and damaged much infrastructure to record-setting blizzards that froze the earth.

What I learned in Iowa is that what happened to the land in one season would inevitably impact the harvest in another season. The crops in Iowa didn't exist just so that drivers and farmers could marvel at their beauty. Instead, what was produced had the assignment of feeding humanity. The crops were on a mission. Healthy marriages are those crops that should serve and "feed" the communities in which they exist.

But how do we move from communal service when our crops are barely surviving? Year after year, situationship after situationship, failed relationship after failed relationship with no harvest is how many of us can describe our dating and mating lives. Real talk, some of us continue to plant the same seeds and we continue to get the same, "It's Complicated" crops. Sister, it may be time to do a soil study (emotional and physical health), a seed study (messages you are consuming), and looking at what you're using to water your crops (behaviors and communication). Oftentimes, these studies require that fields are placed in a state of rest.

As the coronavirus made it even more difficult to casually date or develop meaningful relationships with someone I met at the beginning of the year and others I had attempted to get to know virtually, I came to the conclusion I just needed to "rest my field." There was no good fruit being produced and each encounter could be described as, "low-vibrational" and non-lifegiving.

For some, resting may mean choosing to press pause on a situationship that isn't yielding any fruit while for others rest may mean not responding to those random social media direct messages where you spend hours if not days of messaging that lead to no more than cramped fingers and eye strain. It's likely that "resting your field" may look completely different to you. For some, "resting your field" may mean honestly thinking about how you have been choosing to "knock the cobwebs off" or have casual sex for the sake of maintenance.

I've done that, too, and it's emotionally exhausting, even if you are the best of friends and there is some level of care and love for your partner. Sex is not solely a physical act. While some argue against the theological and spiritual legitimacy of "soul ties," I believe there is a connection to the people or souls you've connected with through sexual intimacy. Call it what you like, but why do we continue to think or possibly even continue to care about people whose phone numbers we have blocked after the court hearing? Sorry, that's for those who have busted windows out of cars, as crooned by Jazmine Sullivan.

Our bodies, or what I consider here as "the field," require the soil to maintain health to sustain what is planted. For example, in the natural, crops can get contaminated due to the runoff from adjacent fields producing waste and other toxic substances. Any future "water" that comes to your land should come to nourish and sustain and not leave you barren.

You can't reap a harvest in any season, and many have tried to reap the harvest of healthy relationships through seasons with unfavorable elements. My prayer is you will take the time to discern and observe times of rest from toxic relationships, casual sex, and any situation that leaves you broke and broken. Oh, I'm on the same journey alongside you.

Resting my field is an intentional act, while I recognize that for many it may be circumstantial. It's possible that you have not been in a romantic relationship or even out on a date in a matter of years. If someone tried to water your field with a touch, you wouldn't even know how to appropriately respond. If you're honest, you may feel like you have been left to rot while others around you are flourishing and dating, getting engaged, or appear to be in fruitful marriages. It's enough to make you want to throw in the towel, get you a cat, and live happily ever after while watching *Gunsmoke* alone each night. You've stopped planting, watering, or expecting a harvest. Beloved, while resting our bodies and emotions may help prepare for the harvest that is yet unseen, my prayer is that you will rest in expectancy.

Rest and hope.

Rest and trust that like Hagar who cried by a spring in the wilderness, you will sense that God sees you. Not only does God see you, but God remembers you. Like Hagar, maybe others have taken advantage of your body and have gotten what they desired from the exchange while you have been left feeling abandoned and despised.

My prayer is that you will know that you are not abandoned, and you are certainly not alone.

Reflection Questions

How have you sown love into others while failing to water your field?

As you consider rest for your body, mind, and soul, what self-care strategies will you use to restore and nourish yourself for the road ahead?

In what areas of your life do you need God to water and restore?

What are the other questions you would like to reflect on as you continue on your journey?
Write them here.

Closing Prayer

Dear God,

God help me forgive myself as you have forgiven me.

I forgive myself for not being the best steward over my body, emotions, and money. I thank you for being the lover of my soul.

I need you to cleanse my thoughts and remove the playback reels of intimacy experienced with lovers who have emotionally and physically moved and have married other women.

Their name is no longer uttered, and phone numbers are blocked, yet I continue to savor the touch of their fingertips, the gentleness of their tongue, and the smell of their essence. Each of those expressions transport me back to a transactional moment that once felt like the biggest deposit of love.

I am now left with an emotional and spiritual deficit. While the memories are sweet and ignite a fire inside, there is also pain that resides in my heart.

As my mind is purged, allow me to feel your Divine presence and touch. At the appointed time when the appointed one you have sent knows me in the marital bed, may there be a clean slate. Do not allow me to bring the expectations of how I was caressed, held, or touched before into this sacred space.

Allow my husband's touch to be the only one I desire and his name to be the only one called out. God, you are concerned about everything concerning me, so I come asking you to reset and restore the parts of me that you created.

Amen and Ase'

Epilogue

Whew, chile!

While many will judge the words deposited on these pages, I took a road called vulnerability because I believe the journey was worth others being liberated. There are enough sanitized testimonies to go around until Jesus returns.

Scripture tells us we "overcome by the words of our testimony," (Revelation 12:11), so my prayer is this book has provided an opportunity for you to begin a strategic diggin' into your own experiences that may have led to love or to loving yourself more fully and embracing the journey that leads to healing and wholeness.

I could have taken all of these stories to the grave, but then those lessons that could lead to someone else's healing would end up in the ground alongside the volumes of books never published. As this book was being completed during the first days of Advent 2020, it became much clearer that this text would set captives free. Jesus came to set captives free.

Those who walk through the world bound by the shame of past sexual encounters and unwelcomed violations must be reminded that they are valuable to God, no matter what. I pray that you embrace the freedom to love your body and seek pleasure that honors God as well as yourself.

Here are ways you can continue the diggin' process:

- Consider psychotherapy to process any matters that may have been triggered while reading this text.

- Consider talking with your current partner about how the intimacy you share can be enhanced or the possible reasons that may cause you to appear withdrawn during lovemaking.

- Talk with trusted friends about the revelations from the book that may be of interest to them. Consider gathering a group of friends to explore the questions at the end of each chapter.

- If there is a safe space to store your words, then begin or continue journaling daily to process your past and current emotions.

- Consult with your spiritual advisor or pastor to explore the questions you may have about your faith and relationship with God.

Pray and ask God to heal broken parts of your heart that you've intentionally hidden for decades because it's just been too difficult to attend to wounds that never healed.

If this book has blessed you, buy a copy for a friend, mention it in social media posts, refer it to your book or reading group, and pray that it continues to bless others.

**Diggin' for Intimacy Playlist
(All songs are available on YouTube and via
other streaming platforms.)**

Songs for Affirmation
Happy Being Me by Angie Stone
I Am Light by India.Arie

Songs for Celebration
Golden by Jill Scott
It's My Time by Kelly Price
Private Party by India.Arie

Songs for Worship
Dear God by Smokie Norful
Withholding Nothing by William McDowell
I'm Still Here by Dorinda Cark Cole

Songs for Faith Building
I'll Trust You by Donnie McClurkin
Trust Me by Richard Smallwood
Worth Fighting For by Brian Courtney
Wilson

Songs for Reaffirming Love
Ready For Love by India.Arie
Teach Me by Musiq Soulchild
Why I Love You by Major

Songs for Restoration
Deliver Me (This Is My Exodus) by Donald Lawrence featuring Le'Andria Johnson
Heal Me by Faith A. Davis
I Won't Go Back by William McDowell
Lord Make Me Over - Tonéx/B. Slade

Resources

Organizations Offering Additional Support

If after reading this book you feel like you need additional support to continue the digging and healing process, then please consider the following organizations that may offer information and support:

Black Mental Wellness:
https://www.blackmentalwellness.com

Melanin and Mental Health:
https://www.melaninandmentalhealth.com

NAMI: https://nami.org

Sex Addicts Anonymous:
http://www.sexaa.org

The Boris Lawrence Henson Foundation:
https://borislhensonfoundation.org/

Therapy for Black Men:
https://therapyforblackmen.org/about/

Will You Be Whole:
https://willyoubewhole.com

Author Bio

The Rev. Dr. Arlecia D. Simmons began her professional career as a newspaper reporter but now communicates on God's behalf as an ordained minister. Simmons is an educator, an award-winning journalist, a playwright, and an inspirational speaker and writer.

Simmons earned a Bachelor of Arts in Mass Communication from Winthrop University and a Master of Arts in Journalism from the University of South Carolina. In December 2009, she earned a Doctor of Philosophy degree in Mass Communications from the University of Iowa while completing her first semester at Duke University Divinity School. She graduated from Duke in May

2012 and was ordained to Christian ministry on Pentecost Sunday, May 27, 2012. The American Baptist Churches USA endorses her ordination. Simmons enjoys educating people about the unique Gullah culture that shaped her identity.

She is a member of Delta Sigma Theta Sorority, Inc., and the National Association of Black Journalists.

Contact the Author

To book the Rev. Dr. Arlecia D. Simmons for speaking engagements, workshops, or writing projects, e-mail her at admin@drlecia.com. Visit her online at https://drlecia.com.